READ WELL Plus

# Dinosaur Clues

**UNITS 49, 50 STORYBOOK**

Copyright 2006 Sopris West Educational Services. All rights reserved.

ISBN 1-59318-511-1

10 09 08 07          4 5 6

**SOPRIS WEST** EDUCATIONAL SERVICES
A CAMBIUM LEARNING COMPANY

BOSTON, MA • LONGMONT, CO

TABLE OF CONTENTS
# UNIT 49 • Dinosaur Life

Planning Assistance: See Daily Lesson Planning for scheduling.

TABLE OF CONTENTS

# UNIT 50 • The Bobosaurus

Planning Assistance: See Daily Lesson Planning for scheduling.

# Dinosaur Life

*By Jessica MacMurray Blaine and Marilyn Sprick*
*Illustrated by Ka Botzis*

## Vocabulary Words

**classify**
> To classify is to put things into groups.
> Scientists classify animals into groups.
> When things are arranged into groups,
> it is called classification.

**extinct**
> To be extinct is to no longer exist.
> Dinosaurs disappeared 65 million years
> ago. They are extinct.

**fossils**
> Fossils are what is left of animals and
> plants that lived long ago. Fossils are
> often as hard as rock. Dinosaur bones
> that were left from millions of years
> ago are fossils.

# UNIT 49 STORIES

# Millions of Years Ago

What are you going to learn about in this unit?

Millions of years ago dinosaurs roamed Earth.

These amazing animals lived on Earth for about 165 million years. Then they disappeared.

Have you ever seen a live dinosaur at school? In a park? In a zoo? Why not? That makes me wonder what happened to the dinosaurs. Why do you think the dinosaurs disappeared?

## Size

Some dinosaurs were enormous animals. Perhaps the biggest dinosaur was Argentinosaurus (Are-jen-TEEN-o-sore-us). It was about 120 feet long—longer than three school buses—and as tall as a six-story building! This dinosaur was so big, scientists think it spent all of its time eating.

If you were as large as an Argentinosaurus, how do you think you would move? I think I would have moved slowly!

Some dinosaurs were very small. The smallest dinosaur we know about was about the size of a cat. It may have been small, but it had a very long name. Try it— Micropachycephalosaurus (My-crow-packy-sef-uh-low-sore-us). It means "little thick-headed lizard."

Describe the largest dinosaur scientists have studied. Describe the smallest dinosaur people have found.

## Movement

Some dinosaurs walked on four legs, like an elephant. Some walked on two legs, like people do. Some even walked on four legs when they were eating, but ran on two legs when they were in danger.

## Appearance

Dinosaurs were fantastic creatures. They came in all shapes and sizes.

- Stegosaurus had two rows of plates running down its back.

- Triceratops had a three-horned face
  and a large, bony frill protecting its neck.
  Imagine wearing three horns and a
  big frill.

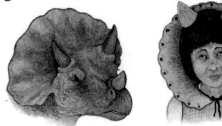

- Duck-billed dinosaurs had odd-shaped
  heads. This duck-billed dinosaur had a
  hollow tube on its head. Scientists think
  the dinosaur hooted through the tube.
  Imagine having a tube on your head!

If you had to choose, which dinosaur would you rather be? Touch the
picture on page 10. What dinosaur is that? Look at page 11. Touch
the Triceratops. Now, touch the duck-billed dinosaur.

# Dinosaur Classification

You know a lot about the way scientists classify animals. Do you think the dinosaurs were mammals?

## Dinosaurs One and All

Dinosaurs were part of the animal kingdom. They came in all shapes and sizes, but they were all one class of animal.

## Were Dinosaurs Mammals?

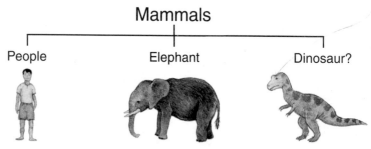

Mammals

People          Elephant          Dinosaur?

Dinosaurs were not mammals. Like mammals, dinosaurs had backbones and took care of their babies. Unlike mammals, dinosaurs did not give live birth to their babies. They laid eggs. Since they laid eggs, perhaps they were birds.

Do you think dinosaurs were birds? Why not?

## **Were Dinosaurs Birds?**

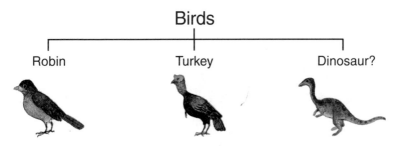

Like birds, dinosaurs had backbones, some had beaks, and they laid eggs. Unlike birds, most dinosaurs did not have feathers. If they weren't birds, perhaps they were amphibians.

Do you think dinosaurs were amphibians? Why not?

## Were Dinosaurs Amphibians?

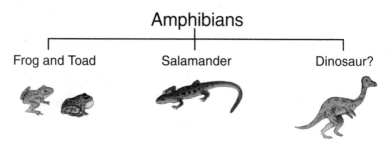

Amphibians

Frog and Toad     Salamander     Dinosaur?

Dinosaurs were not amphibians. Scientists think they may have been cold-blooded, but unlike frogs and toads, dinosaurs never lived in the water, and they did not go through a metamorphosis.

## Reptiles

Dinosaurs were reptiles. They are related to snakes, crocodiles, turtles, and lizards. In fact, the word "dinosaur" means "terrible lizard." Like other reptiles, most dinosaurs had scaly skin, laid eggs, were cold-blooded, and breathed air with their lungs.

# Reptiles

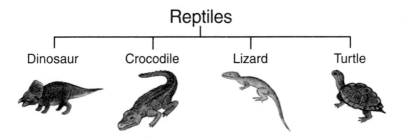

| Dinosaur | Crocodile | Lizard | Turtle |

How are dinosaurs classified? Were they mammals? Birds? Amphibians? How do you know? Are there any dinosaurs alive today? Read the next chapter to find out what dinosaur babies were like.

# Dinosaur Eggs

Turtles, lizards, snakes, and crocodiles all lay eggs, and so did the dinosaurs.

## Small Eggs

Some dinosaurs were huge. Some dinosaurs were small. But surprisingly, none of their eggs were very big. The largest eggs were only about one foot long—about the size of a football.

## <u>Nests and Eggs</u>

Dinosaur mothers made nests, just like birds do. Dinosaurs made their nests in the ground. The dinosaur mother would hollow out a soft place or make a mound and lay her eggs. Sometimes, more than one mother would lay eggs in the same nest. Dinosaur mothers would take turns protecting their eggs, just like a big family.

What did you learn about dinosaur nests and eggs?

## Hatching

Inside the eggs, baby dinosaurs grew until they were ready to hatch. Then, each baby would use a special tooth to break its egg.

Some baby dinosaurs stayed in the nest for a while after they were born. The mother dinosaur would protect them and bring them food until they were ready to go out on their own.

How were dinosaurs like birds? Some scientists think dinosaurs may have been related to birds.

## Growing

Some baby dinosaurs were so small, they could fit in your hand. But they would grow quickly. Scientists think some dinosaurs gained as much as 100 pounds per day. They would grow to be as big as a dog, then as big as a car, then as big as a house!

I think it is strange that a dinosaur could hatch out of an egg as small as a football and grow to be as big as a building. You learned some amazing facts about dinosaurs.

# Dinosaur Dinner

You've learned a lot about dinosaurs. What's the title of this selection? What would you like to learn about dinosaur dinners?

## Meat Eaters (Carnivores)

Some dinosaurs ate only other animals. They ate other dinosaurs, birds, fish, and even insects. (Some insects were huge. Dragonflies were as large as seagulls.)

Why would dragonflies have made a good dinosaur dinner?

Tyrannosaurus Rex

Meat eaters spent their days hunting. Some had big heads, strong legs, and short arms. The meat eaters would kill other animals. Then they would eat the animal with their sharp teeth.

What facts did we learn about the meat eaters?

Tyrannosaurus Rex is the most famous of the meat eaters. This creature was as tall as a two-story house. It had powerful jaws and huge teeth—up to seven inches long.

## Plant Eaters (Herbivores)

Many of the biggest dinosaurs didn't eat meat. They were peaceful plant eaters. Plant eaters spent their days eating the leaves of trees, flowers, grasses, and shrubs.

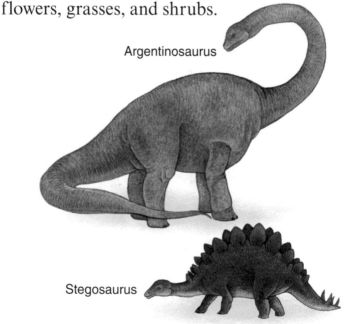

Argentinosaurus

Stegosaurus

Argentinosaurus, Stegosaurus, Hadrosaurus, and Triceratops were all herbivores.

Plant eaters came in all shapes and sizes. Argentinosaurus (Are-jen-TEEN-o-sore-us) was a plant eater. Stegosaurus, Triceratops, and the duck-billed dinosaurs were all plant eaters.

Hadrosaurus

Triceratops

Plant eaters had to protect themselves from the meat eaters.

Look at the pictures. Name the four plant eaters. How do you think these dinosaurs protected themselves?

Some plant eaters were simply too big for the meat eaters to attack. Other plant eaters had horns and spikes. One dinosaur had a crest on its head that it used like a horn. When a meat-eating dinosaur was near, this strange dinosaur could warn others by hooting through its crest.

What facts did we learn about the plant eaters?

## **Plant and Animal Eaters (Omnivores)**

Different dinosaurs had different ways of living. Some dinosaurs were not carnivores or herbivores. Like people, some dinosaurs ate both plants *and* animals.

Gallimimus was an omnivore.

I think it would be fun to have a dinosaur pet. If dinosaurs were still living, which dinosaur would you want for a pet? A meat eater? A plant eater? Or an omnivore?

## Dinosaur Discoveries

Brachiosaurus

Dinosaurs have been extinct for 65 million years. No one has ever seen a live dinosaur. Yet, we know that the dinosaur in the picture was about 70 feet long and about as tall as a four-story building. We know it lived in herds and had to keep moving most of the day to find food.

Since no one has ever seen a living dinosaur, how do we know so much about these animals?

What facts do you know about Brachiosaurus?

Even though the dinosaurs died out, they left behind clues.

## Dinosaur Bones

When some dinosaurs died, their bodies were covered by mud and sand. The soft body parts rotted away. Over time, the bones turned to stone. The dinosaur bones became fossils. Dinosaur bones tell us a lot about dinosaurs— how big they were, how they moved, and even how they protected themselves.

When bones turn to stone, what are they called? What have scientists learned from fossils?

## Footprints

Some dinosaurs left behind footprints that hardened in the mud. By studying footprints, scientists have learned that some dinosaurs traveled in herds. These dinosaurs protected their young by keeping them in the center of the herd.

Scientists use clues to figure out how the dinosaurs lived. What did they find out from ancient footprints? I think it's very interesting that dinosaurs lived in herds like sheep or cows. They also must have been good parents.

## Dinosaur Eggs

Scientists love finding dinosaur eggs. Sometimes small skeletons remain inside the eggs for scientists to study. Dinosaur eggs have been found in about 200 places around the world. On a hillside in China, a farmer found a huge dinosaur nest with at least 26 eggs. It was a very exciting day for the farmer. It was an exciting day for scientists.

Dinosaur fossils have been found all over the world. Imagine finding a dinosaur fossil!

What would you do if you found a dinosaur fossil?

# Unit 49 Glossary

**carnivores**
>Animals that eat meat are called carnivores.

**classify**
>To classify is to put things into groups.
>Scientists classify animals into groups.

**dinosaur**
>A dinosaur is an extinct reptile that lived millions of years ago.

**extinct**
>To be extinct is to no longer exist.
>Dinosaurs disappeared 65 million years ago. They are extinct.

**fossils**
>Fossils are what is left of animals and plants that lived long ago. Fossils are often as hard as rock.

# Unit 49 Glossary (*continued*)

**herbivores**
> Animals that eat plants are called herbivores.

**lizards**
> Lizards are reptiles that have dry, scaly skin and love to get warm in the sun.

**omnivores**
> Animals that eat both meat and plants are called omnivores.

**reptiles**
> Reptiles are cold-blooded animals that have scaly skin, lay eggs, and breathe air with their lungs.

**scientist**
> A scientist is a person who studies things by looking for clues and making guesses.

# Storybook Decoding Review

**Sounds and words you can read:**

| | | | |
|---|---|---|---|
| b<u>oy</u> | h<u>au</u>l | n<u>oi</u>se | r<u>oa</u>d |
| m<u>oa</u>n | t<u>oy</u> | <u>oi</u>l | P<u>au</u>l |
| v<u>oi</u>ce | f<u>au</u>lt | j<u>oy</u> | p<u>oi</u>nt |

**Words you can sound out:**

| | | | |
|---|---|---|---|
| family | engine | study | surprise |
| classify | reptile | largest | peaceful |
| remain | nation | below | bony |

**Words you can read:**

| | | | |
|---|---|---|---|
| creature | break | special | lizard |
| against | moved | groups | piece |

**Phrases you can read:**

Better late than never.

Practice what you preach.

**Sentences you can read:**

Scientists classify animals into groups.

The word "dinosaur" means "terrible lizard."

Dinosaurs no longer exist, so they are extinct.

# The Bobosaurus

*By Beau Pritchart and Jessica Sprick*
*Illustrated by Ashley Mims*

## Vocabulary Words

**extinct**
To be extinct is to no longer exist.
Dinosaurs disappeared 65 million years
ago. They are extinct.

**fossils**
Fossils are what is left of animals and
plants that lived long ago. Fossils are
often as hard as rock. Dinosaur bones
that were left from millions of years
ago are fossils.

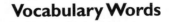

# UNIT 50 STORY

## The Bobosaurus

## The Bobosaurus

## CHAPTER 1

### The Muddy Walk

We think "The Bobosaurus" is going to be about a dinosaur. You already know a lot about dinosaurs. If Bobosaurus is a dinosaur, what do you already know about it?

Paul loved to take his dog, Bobo, on long walks. Each day, Paul and Bobo would go to the end of town to walk along the edge of the forest.

Sometimes Paul heard strange noises coming from the dark forest. He was afraid of the forest, but it was fun to peek into the wet trees. Paul wondered what might be lurking in the dark.

It had been raining for days and days. When the rain finally stopped, Paul and Bobo were excited to go exploring. Paul pulled on his boots. He put Bobo on his leash, and they headed out for a muddy walk.

Imagine going on a walk after it has rained a lot. How would the air feel?

Paul's parents had warned him not to let Bobo off his leash. They said Bobo would run away into the forest, but Bobo never went far from Paul's side. When they got to the edge of town, Paul would take Bobo off the leash.

But this time, when Paul let Bobo go free, the dog headed straight for the forest. Paul yelled, "Bobo, come here!" Bobo turned and barked twice at Paul. Then he headed into the forest and disappeared.

Paul could hear Bobo barking in the distance, but Bobo was nowhere in sight. Paul stood at the edge of the forest calling, "Bobo, Bobo!" Still, the dog did not come back.

Look at Paul. What's his problem? How do you think he feels? Why didn't Paul run after Bobo? Paul thought there might be things *lurking* in the forest. What do you think "lurking" means?

## CHAPTER 2

### Into the Forest

Who is the story about?  What is Paul's problem?

Paul was worried.  Bobo had disappeared into the dark forest.  Paul had called and called.  It wasn't like Bobo to run off.  Paul wasn't sure what to do.  He was afraid to go into the forest.  Paul thought, "I know who can help—Alexis!"

Paul's older sister, Alexis, was twelve.  Paul knew she would be able to find Bobo.  Paul sprinted home.  He threw open the door to his house.  Alexis was sprawled on the couch, reading a book about dinosaurs.  She was very smart and was always reading.

Alexis said, "Paul, did you know that some dinosaurs were as big as a six-story house?"  She looked up.  Paul gasped for breath and pointed to the forest.

Paul gasped for breath.  Show me what that means.  Why was he out of breath?

Who is the new character in the story? What do you know about
Alexis? Do you think Alexis will help Paul find Bobo? What do you
think Alexis and Paul will do next?

When Paul caught his breath, he explained that Bobo was in the forest. Alexis pulled on her boots. She grabbed Paul's hand, and they ran to the forest. Paul started to say he didn't want to go in, but Alexis dragged him through the wall of trees.

It was dark in the forest. Strange noises came from all around them. Alexis began calling for Bobo. Alexis and Paul heard an excited bark. They began running toward the sound.

Imagine yourself in a dark forest with strange noises all around you. Would you worry about wild animals lurking in the dark? How would you feel? I think Paul and Alexis were very scared. How do you think they felt when they heard Bobo's bark?

## CHAPTER 3
### The Mudslide

Who is the story about?  What are they trying to do?

Alexis and Paul were running.  They were getting closer and closer to the sound of the barking dog.

Paul looked at the dark trees around him as he ran.  Paul wasn't watching Alexis.  When she stopped, Paul ran SMACK into her.  Paul started to say, "Watch it!"  But then he saw why Alexis had stopped.

The ground had given way from all of the rain.  A big mudslide had made a cliff right in front of them!

Close your eyes and imagine a big mudslide in the forest.  Imagine standing at the edge of a cliff.  How would you feel?

Alexis and Paul heard a muffled bark. Bobo appeared with what looked like a stick in his mouth. Alexis bent down and scolded Bobo for running away. Then she grabbed the stick to throw it for him.

Before she could throw it, Alexis stopped. There was something odd about the stick. Alexis began looking closely at it, and then she let out a whoop. "Paul, look at this! I think Bobo's found a bone. But it's not like any bone I've ever seen."

Alexis looked over at Paul, but he was just staring at the mudslide. "What is it?" Alexis asked. Paul pointed to the mud below. Alexis peered over the edge of the cliff and saw more of the strange-looking sticks poking out of the mud.

Look at the sticks poking up from the mud. What do you think Bobo and the kids found? If the bones are dinosaur bones, what do you already know about them?

# CHAPTER 4

## The Big Find

Who are the main characters?  What was the problem at the beginning of the story?  What did the children do to find Bobo?  What do you think they found?

Alexis and Paul made their way down through the mud to the huge sticks.  As they got closer, they saw that some of the sticks were three or four times taller than they were!

Alexis looked closely at the bones.  She said, "Paul, we've found a dinosaur!  Look at the head!"  She pointed to the skull.  Paul was so excited, he couldn't say anything.  Bobo barked, wagged his tail, and picked up another bone.

Alexis and Paul wanted to tell their parents about their discovery.  Paul put Bobo on his leash.  Alexis picked up one of the bones.  Then they hurried home.

Imagine discovering dinosaur bones.  How old do you think the fossils were?

At first, Alexis and Paul's parents didn't know what to think of the bones. They started making phone calls. Soon, there were people everywhere. There were scientists with fancy equipment. There were television people with cameras. There were neighbors with no clue about what was going on!

The scientists said the giant bones were from a dinosaur. It was a kind of dinosaur that no one had ever found before! More scientists began coming from all over the world to study the bones.

What did Alexis and Paul's parents do? What happened next? How do you think everyone felt? Why did scientists come from all over the world? What are dinosaur bones called?

Look at the fossils in the picture. What kind of dinosaur do you think Bobo and the kids found? What do you think the scientists will do?

## CHAPTER 5

### Bobo's Bones

Paul, Alexis, and Bobo had the most exciting summer of their lives. They were on TV. They were in newspapers and magazines. Headlines read, "BOBO'S BONES—The Most Exciting Find in Years"!

Paul and Alexis made a scrapbook with all of the stories from the newspapers and magazines. Their scrapbook was filled with pictures of the scientists uncovering the bones. There were also pictures of Paul and Alexis cleaning dirt off the bones.

There were pictures in the scrapbook of Bobo trying to steal the dinosaur bones. (The scientists wouldn't let him pick up the bones anymore, because they didn't want him to leave teeth marks. They gave Bobo dog treats instead.)

Why do you think they made a scrapbook?

If you found dinosaur fossils, what would you put in your scrapbook? Use the word "extinct" to explain why the dinosaur discovery was so exciting.

In a television interview, Paul and Alexis both announced that they wanted to be scientists when they grew up. Paul said he wanted to find more dinosaur fossils. Alexis said she wanted to travel all over the world to look for more dinosaur bones.

The most exciting news of the summer was when the scientists named the dinosaur. Newspaper headlines read, "Bobosaurus— Doggie's Dino Gets a Name."

What did the scientists name the dinosaur? Do you think Bobo was excited about having the dinosaur named after him? Who do you think was excited?

# CHAPTER 6

## The Scrapbook

Who are the main characters? Why were Paul, Alexis, and Bobo in the news? This chapter is about Paul and Alexis's scrapbook.

What do you think will be inside the scrapbook?

# DOG DIGS UP DINOSAUR BONES

By Roy Reporter

A dog found a dinosaur skeleton yesterday in the small town of Mudland.

Bobo, the dog, found the bones while on a long walk. His owners, Alexis and Paul, said that Bobo brought them a bone and then took them to the rest of the skeleton.

"We are so proud of Bobo," said Alexis. "He is a wonderful dog!"

Scientists are still not sure what kind of dinosaur was found.

The unknown dinosaur . . .

What is the headline in this story? Why is Bobo becoming famous? Use the word "discovered" in your answer. What interesting fact did the reporter write about the dinosaur?

# FANTASTIC FIND IN DINO DIG
## A NEW KIND OF DINOSAUR IS DISCOVERED

By Joyce Tellall

Scientists said that the dinosaur bones discovered last week are from a dinosaur that has never been found before.

Scientist Donny Digger said, "It has been years since anyone has found a new dinosaur. Bobo's discovery is the most exciting find in years!"

## The Dinosaur With No Name!

This is another reporter's story. What is her headline? Do you think the dinosaur was a fantastic discovery? Why?

Look at all of the great pictures in the scrapbook. Let's look at each one and see if we can tell what it shows.

# BOBOSAURUS—
## DOGGIE'S DINO GETS A NAME
By Roy Reporter

Scientists have decided on a name for the new dinosaur that was found in Mudland weeks ago.

The dinosaur will be named Bobosaurus. The name comes from the dog, Bobo, that first found the dinosaur bones.

## The Dinosaur Bobo Found— It's a Bobosaurus!!

What's the headline in this story? This story is also by Roy Reporter. It tells why the dinosaur was named Bobosaurus. Who was the dinosaur named after?

# THE BOBOSAURUS

◆ Who was the story about?
Where did the story take place?

● What happened at the beginning of the story?
Try to use the word "lurking."

■ What happened in the middle of the story?
Try to use the words "discover" and "discovery."

▲ What happened at the end of the story? Try to use the words "fossils" and "extinct."

# Unit 50 Glossary

**dinosaur**

> A dinosaur is an extinct reptile that lived millions of years ago.

**discover**

> To discover is to see or find out something for the first time.

**extinct**

> To be extinct is to no longer exist.
> Dinosaurs have died out, so they are extinct.

**fossils**

> Fossils are what is left of animals and plants that lived long ago. Fossils are often as hard as rock.

**lurking**

> If something is lurking, it is hiding and seems dangerous.

**scientist**

> A person who studies and observes things is a scientist.

# Storybook Decoding Review

✏️ **Sound Review:**

| | | | |
|---|---|---|---|
| fawn | few | crow | change |
| cent | know | phone | float |
| voice | launch | giant | boy |

✈️ **Words you can sound out:**

| | | | |
|---|---|---|---|
| enjoy | fudge | explain | astronaut |
| sprinted | noise | playful | famous |
| children | unknown | unsafe | disappear |

⬤ **Words you have learned:**

| | | | |
|---|---|---|---|
| through | covered | worried | idea |
| break | neighbors | certain | piece |

♥ **Phrases you can read:**

Easier said than done.

Keep your fingers crossed.

■ **Sentences you can read:**

In the beginning, Bobo went into the forest.

In the middle, the children found dinosaur bones.

In the end, the dinosaur was named after Bobo.